REALITY CHECK

BOOKS BY DENNIS O'DRISCOLL

POETRY

Reality Check
New and Selected Poems
Exemplary Damages
Weather Permitting
Quality Time
Long Story Short
Hidden Extras
Kist

ESSAYS

Troubled Thoughts, Majestic Dreams

INTERVIEWS

Stepping Stones: Interviews with Seamus Heaney

AS EDITOR

Quote Poet Unquote
The Bloodaxe Book of Poetry Quotations

REALITY CHECK

DENNIS O'DRISCOLL

COPPER CANYON PRESS
PORT TOWNSEND, WASHINGTON

Cover art: Patrick Scott, *MP4*, 2006. Gold leaf, palladium, and acrylic on linen, 61 x 61 cm. Courtesy of the artist and Taylor Galleries, Dublin. Photograph by Richard Kingston.

Copper Canyon Press is in residence at Fort Worden State Park in Port Townsend, Washington, under the auspices of Centrum. Centrum is a gathering place for artists and creative thinkers from around the world, students of all ages and backgrounds, and audiences seeking extraordinary cultural enrichment.

LIBRARY OF CONGRESS CATALOGING-IN-PUBLICATION DATA
O'Driscoll, Dennis.
  Reality check / Dennis O'Driscoll.
    p. cm.
  Poems.
  ISBN 978-1-55659-280-5 (pbk. : alk. paper)
  I. Title.

PR6065.D75R43 2008
821´.914—dc22

                                        2008014583

98765432 FIRST PRINTING

COPPER CANYON PRESS
Post Office Box 271
Port Townsend, Washington 98368
www.coppercanyonpress.org

ACKNOWLEDGMENTS

Grateful acknowledgment is made to the editors of the following, where some of the poems in this collection were first published: *Five Points*, the *Irish Times*, *Parnassus*, *PN Review*, *Poetry Daily*, *Poetry Review*, and the *Times Literary Supplement*.

An earlier version of "Fifty O'Clock" was published by The Happy Dragons Press (Essex) as a limited-edition chapbook, edited by Shirley Toulson and printed by Julius Stafford-Baker. Three poems in the collection appeared in *All the Living*, a limited-edition book edited by Thomas Dillon Redshaw and printed by Paulette Myers-Rich at Traffic Street Press (Minnesota). "Diversions" was commissioned by Declan Meade for the 2006 Oxfam calendar.

Profound thanks to J. Patrick Lannan and Lannan Foundation, the American Academy of Arts and Letters, and Lawrence O'Shaughnessy and the Center for Irish Studies of the University of St. Thomas for their support and encouragement.

CONTENTS

REALITY CHECK

PART ONE

Diversions

Lean on the green recycle bin
    in the yard where roses run amok,
scent intensified by last night's rain.

Lift your eyes to the sunlit hills: hedge-
    perforated fields are first-day issues
tweezered askew in your childhood album.

Rest on the laurels of your elbows.
    Consent to mind and body going
their ways amicably, a trial separation.

Even the distant glimpse of a dozen
    hormone-puffed cattle can sometimes
be enough to raise your spirits from their rut.

Or an uncouth stream—only slightly
    the worse for farm waste—topped up
from some unfathomable source.

You ache to touch the hem of its current
    as you drive by, reach out like a willow leaf,
contrive a way, in passing, to partake.

Cassandra

after Hans Magnus Enzensberger

For years, all we showed
    her for her pains
were two deaf ears,
    as she fumed over
global warming,
    emitting dire predictions
in her smoky voice:
    catastrophic floods, etc.,
high-rise high-rent condos
    marinating in brine...
Though we'd buried
    our heads for ages
like spent fuel rods,
    her prophecies are
a hot topic suddenly
    on every chat show.
There's not a taxi driver
    who can't repeat
her words like racehorse
    tips, a dead cert.
Her rumours spread
    at hurricane speed.
Her hoarse phrases
    —"before long," "too late"—
sink in at last.

Hang on a minute, though.
How many years does
"before long" add up to?

How late is "too late"?
How up-to-date is she on
current scientific R & D?

We carry on as bravely as we can
in these uncertain times:
4x4s at every door.

Low-fare airlines for cheap access
to nest-egg second houses.
All-year strawberries in supermarkets.

BUSINESS AS USUAL signs
displayed on hoardings everywhere,
with so much construction underway.

Bread and Butter

The rich abundance of the still-life
        painter's palette: glistening
pitchers; pewter kitchenware
        battered like windfallen fruit;
fatted watermelons, grapes
        and apricots; bushy heads
of cauliflower in season.
        And sweetmeats. And bread.
Bread that no more has
        a season than the air;
keeping bakers awake all night
        worrying over loaves.
A corner is nicked from this roll
        painted with eggshell delicacy;
maybe the artist, unable to desist,
        picked absentmindedly at
the burnished crust, as when
        a restaurant diner—all eyes
on the menu—fumbles with
        the basket of plaited rolls.

$\sim$

Where to start? Remembered batch pans wrapped
like exquisite gifts in tissue paper when you were
despatched townward on your bike for a family loaf.
Mushy white sliced in waxed Coady's Bakery packaging.
Homemade brown soda, rough and ready, signed off
with a dividing cross, yet reconciling divergent elements—
salt, buttermilk, baking soda, wholemeal flour—devising
a viable compromise among them all. A harvest loaf with
ornamental bark to carve through and reveal its inner grain,
leaving a trail of crumbs, like sawdust, on the breadboard.

Char-marked nan, flat as blini pancakes, chewy as pizza
base, coriander-enhanced, ghee-brushed, Sri Lanka–shaped.
Unconsecrated hosts, surplus to the church's needs, doled out
by the school nun, savoured as a wafery ambrosian appetiser.
Brie-like wheels of flour-dusted sourdough—moist of crumb
and crisp of crust—cooling on the wire racks of a coffee shop
the time you stopped in pastel-painted clapboard Telluride.
The over-the-top iced raisin-and-walnut loaf your mother
loved to embellish further with a coating of lime marmalade.
Toast the moment of surrender when the fat hits the pan
and you yield to the full breakfast experience—bacon, sausage,
pudding, field mushrooms, potato cakes—mopping up
egg seepage with a dripping dodge of well-fried bread.
Exotic morning offerings, topped with poppy seeds, fortified
with sun-dried tomatoes, you first sampled with bureaucratic
caution at the Euroflat Hotel in the EU *quartier* of Bruxelles.
All the slices of life bread has treated you to...

Fast-moving, computer-clock-watching, speed-dating
Ireland in its high-tech phase digests its daily bread as rapidly
as text messages, or chews it over at a lunchtime desk
with an urgent request for a ballpark profits forecast.
Office juniors form a breadline for chilli pesto rosso,
baba ghanoush, baby spinach, yellow peppers on ciabatta.
Then the tough decisions: Chai latte? Mocha macchiato?
Best stick strictly to your health regimen: frosty fruits
smoothie, organic Caesar salad wrap, plastic tub
of watercolour melon chunks, detox glass of wheatgrass.

Irish taste buds configured in the bread-and-butter
era, the donkey-cart-to-creamery age that no longer
dares to speak its shabby name, shamefully hunger

sometimes for the old values of the ham sandwich
in a scruffy lunch-hour pub: fat-framed meat in oval
slices, pink folds arrayed on greaseproof paper,
ready, at the half-twelve rush, to be sandwiched with
a wedge of processed cheddar, a slobbery tomato ring
lobbed in for good measure, a tattered lettuce leaf
revived under a cold water tap; white-sliced pan
of pre-focaccia, pre-tortilla days, buttered up incautiously
by the wheezing, plum-faced, sleeve-rolled barman;
cracked plate slapped down—take or leave it—
on a sudsy Guinness beermat. The great mainstay.
Plain or toasted. Pressed into service too with thermos
flask of home-brewed tea for a quick roadside elevenses
between house calls: the salty ham boiled or roasted,
mustard-boosted, pale or wood-smoked; rarest of all,
the joint reserved for special occasions—Christmas,
christenings—honey-glazed, clove-studded, carved thickly
from the bone, ridged with a kitchen knife's serrations.

The butter must be very good in Ireland.
When my American friend spread the word
butter on a hot Santa Fe day, her "butta,"
liberated from flat-earth Irish gutturals, roundly
pronounced its curvature, emphasised the *butt.*
And, as a knob of solid sun was melted down
for heat above deserted New Mexico streets,
a cool grey Irish day flashed nostalgically
to mind: a lunchtime nip out to the bakery
for a crust-flaking demi baguette,
an oven-warm sultana-implanted scone,
three foil-wrapped butter portions.
I see a Tipperary meadow, cows
flinching from insects, fly-whisk tails

patrolling dung-encrusted hindquarters...
Imagination, straying further, reaches
a misty autumn morning, hassocky grass,
spectral shadows, congealed cowpats:
right time and place for moulded cups
of mushrooms to reveal themselves
abruptly, as though parachuted to my feet.
Take some home for breakfast.
Stuff to the gills with chopped herbs.
Smear with garlic butter.
Sear to a tanned hide on the stove lid.
Toast some doughy muffins.
Fan the flames.

∾

Could anyone not
live contentedly on bread
and butter alone?

Crowd Scene

It's like watching a film.

Wisława Szymborska, "The Terrorist, He's Watching"

Warm weather has brought out a good crowd.
They are everything I could have hoped for:
forming orderly queues, scooping up globes
of ice cream, calmly streaming in and out of shops,
checking purses for what spending power is left.

Both sexes, all age groups are represented fairly
among these extras. A pedestrianised street is perfect
for my needs; and how controlled those people are,
all here voluntarily, not one betraying the least
hint of resentment at what is scheduled next.

Hard to grudge some pride that things
are panning out exactly as I'd plotted,
that the capacity gathering is faithful to my plan.
I could embrace them, they are so accommodating,
as if they know they serve a greater cause.

All that will remain, when I have slipped away,
is for the coded statement to be issued through
a trusted channel: screens will flash with breaking news,
shreds of ashen evidence be sifted; the rattled government,
caught off guard, will find holes blown in its defences.

Having rehearsed the details of this crowd scene
so often in my mind, it seems already starting
to vanish into the past. Now let the future arrive.
Today's turnout could not remotely be improved on.
They are having the time of their lives.

And on What

and on what
presumption
parents
may one ask
do you blithely
give life
act as catalyst
for future
generations
grant your
bodily urgings
precedence
over mind
blind impulse
sweeping
reason away
in a surge
of preconceptions
your creative juices
frustrating inhibition
obscuring
the margin
of error
between
your instinct
for survival
and your
perpetuation
of death's
lineage

Intercession

God and humankind meet on uncommon ground.
They just don't speak the same language.

He plays hard to get.
They try to smoke Him from His lair with incense.

They flatter Him with glittering vestments, prayerful
patter, gilded portraits, po-faced processions.

Both sides operate to incompatible agendas.
Priestly mediation fails to close the widening rift.

Their loudest pleas, tempered by
musical settings, fall on His deaf ears.

No, they can't hear what He is saying either.
No, they can't see His side of the story.

The generation gap that separates them
reaches back to the pre-galactic universe.

He thinks in terms of infinity.
They urge research to prolong human life.

He casts His pearly gates before a chosen few.
Before the rest, He raises hell.

His commands are not their wish.
They yearn for riches, youth and beauty.

He bestows gifts of osteitis, earthquakes, infant deaths.
They shake their fists, proclaim their disbelief.

The Call

When we call on God, we always find him out,
away on business maybe, lost in a world of his own,
performing miracles for distant universes, volunteering
to undergo humiliation all over again on another planet's
equivalent of a cross to which his credulous disciples
nail their colours as a drowning man clings to a mast.

He is otherwise engaged perpetually—lines busy;
no menu of options offering access to the top—
his supplicants fobbed off with white-collar staff,
parochial-minded men handling his clients like constituents;
clerical workers undertaking to pass on petitions, insisting
the final decisions fall totally outside their sphere.

We are disillusioned by this failure to meet us face-
to-face, his abdication from fair play when all we ask
is mercy for patients sweltering feverishly through blue
surgical gowns, a softening of his line on chronic pain,
repeal of whatever law ordains that those dealt a poor
hand must suffer the consequences for life, a birth scar.

Is it conceivable that he still dotes on the very hairs
of our sceptical heads, eavesdrops on every arbitrary
phrase, like some benign celestial Nicolae Ceaușescu?
Or is he no longer on speaking terms with mankind,
dismissive of the species as a bad day's work, leading
his campaign trail to more docile outposts of his empire?

Has he ceased believing in his mission statement, lost faith
in his epoch-creating role? Can this universe have spun out
of his control, his conglomerate diversified so much that
a personal touch, a hands-on customer service, is unviable?

We want him to summon a mass gathering like an extraordinary
meeting of shareholders, feed facts to the multitudes this time.

If he has died, where are the oozing wounds to which our doubting
fingers can be applied? What are the chances he may rise again?
Once, his beatific smile graced all our houses like an ancestral
photograph or the graven image of a charismatic president or king.
Now the blanched patch left in its place must be brushed out,
the wall painted over, a hall mirror found to occupy that space.

After Harvest

Tanked up with grain,
the armoured high-
and-mighty combine
harvester discharged
its barley into trailers
and left the field
to tractors, balers.

Polished-off acres
of striped gold
could be a newly laid
timber floor: more like
a pristine showhouse
now than a field as
old as the hills.

An Ulster Landscape

The Old Callan Bridge

John Luke, 1945

Impossible to treat this
postwar idyll—hedged off
from the real world—
seriously at first glance.

The July day is baked
to perfection by the sun;
warm stones in twisty,
cobbled-together roads

batched like bread rolls.
Every wish has met its
match. The bridge with
a river to cool its arches.

The horse with copious
oats. The cows with
grazing on demand.
The hatted man and

grandson who take
to country ways in
summer's marching season.
The dog chasing

children chasing friends.
Hard though it is,
realistically, to place much
faith in the painter's

vision of an Ulster
eternally untroubled,
he still submits his
testimony as credible.

This is the gospel truth
according to John Luke.

All Over Ireland

Snow was general all over Ireland.

James Joyce, "The Dead"

What's general all over Ireland is definitely not snow. Sandbag-
bulky clouds, about to splurge on rain, close in sulkily on all
four provinces, allowing them no quarter, flushing them out.

Rain adds layers of flab to the river where anglers in oilskins
prospect for trout. A downpour drowns the banter of two neighbours.
A course inspection at Leopardstown leads to cancellation.

Rain climbs hills on which foot-rot sheep, dipped in precipitation,
graze with a lamb or two in tow. Rain, not snow, is what blurs
perspectives at furze-lined tourist beauty spots in Kerry and Mayo.

Rain meaning whatever was sent to torment the couple lugging
home a heavy bag of groceries, each grasping a plastic handle.
Rain not snow. On a ruined castle crumbling like a water biscuit.

On a heifer lying low with her drooling mouth full. On a mangy stray.
On a blinking lake. On roofs where zinc tanks corrode and starlings
practise courtship rites. On a night nurse in the sodium-lit carpark.

The man shouldering a wicker basket of racing pigeons to the station
takes a beating from the rain, as do the sleek racehorses making
a run for it in the beech-hedged grounds of sheikh-owned studs.

Rain is general too in the village near the landfill quarry:
it's pensions day in the sub–post office; the creaking door
of a derelict thatched cottage plays second fiddle to a gale.

Rain joins isolated farms where border collies cap each
other's barks, like gossip passed from mouth to mouth. Rain
plinks on the glass dome shielding plastic roses on a grave.

It touches the raw nerves of gaudy window boxes, drums liquid
fingers on the corrugated transit warehouse where cattle destined
for live export to dry Libya or Egypt await their marching orders.

It tries the patience of a foreign film crew hoping the sun will wriggle
out from cloud, and the lodger for whom a limp window-envelope
marked DON'T DELAY!—SAVE MONEY NOW! is the day's only mail.

Rain hammers the builders' hut as a bricklayer shuffles the deck.
Damp patches taint the Old School Restaurant and the Rectory
B & B. Drains back up in the side-street panel-beater's yard.

Rain, bombarding windows, pours out its feelings to a room where
a blue screen saver flickers like a gas flame and a youth revises
for the Garda exam. It throws cold water on a bridal photo shoot.

The minimum-wage man expertly meshing empty supermarket
trolleys is well used to the rain. So too is whoever arranges
the optimistic beach ball and bucket display at the seafront kiosk.

Tub-thumping rain, snubbing the prayers of grain farmers, finds
a welcome in the striped metal barrel at the downpipe and tops
the highest-ever levels measured at Belmullet since records began.

Commuters rush from the bus as if fleeing a catastrophe. Some wear
soaked newspapers as headgear. A woman, doggedly taking her
constitutional by the golf links, pauses under the awning of an oak.

Rain pesters the baffled Latvian au pair on the deserted platform
who fumbles for her contact number. It droppeth on the church hall
that is now a lottery-aided heritage centre for a town down on its luck.

The breadman delivering catering pans to the electroplating unit's
canteen has never seen such rain. Not since yesterday at least
when it seeped through the felt on his flat-roof kitchen extension.

The pelt of the Atlantic Ocean receives the rain like a protective
spray on a pair of crocodile tassel loafers. A brightly pegged
row of tracksuit bottoms sags on a housing estate clothesline.

Tomorrow, yet again, instead of snow the forecast will hold out
the promise of *a dull day everywhere, with rain and drizzle,*
cloud formations like the tissue of a compulsive handwasher's brain.

Rain is general all over Ireland. It lashes the glass panels of the James
Joyce Bridge. Falls on the house where Bartell D'Arcy's song caused
grief one distant Christmas. And upon all the living and the dead.

The Clock

With only one story to tell, the clock strikes
a monotonous note, irrespective of how
musical the bell, how gilded the chimes
its timely conclusions report through.
Time literally on hands, it informs you
to your face exactly where you stand
in relation to your aspirations, stacks up
the odds against your long-term prospects,
leaves your hopes and expectations checked.
Keeping track of time to the last second, it gives
the lie to all small talk about your reputedly
youthful looks, sees through the subterfuge
of dyed hair, exposes the stark truth beneath
the massaged evidence of smooth skin.

Reality Check

i. Death

Death does not come cheap
and is paid for in lumpectomies.
In bone marrow skimmed from relatives.
In sterile hardware ransacking soft parts.

In the clamped aorta of the donor heart.
In students poking round a tube-occluded bed.
How precious death must be to make such
vast demands, exact such satisfaction.

ii. Consultation

What you want to hear him say is,
Nothing to worry about—it's perfectly normal.
What you hear him say is, *I'm afraid…*
grounds for concern…high-risk age group.

What you want to hear him say is,
It's quite routine—it will soon clear up.
What you hear him say is, *The biopsy results*
are back and I won't beat about the bush…

iii. Observation

Every attempt at escape is thwarted here,
the waverings of the heart monitored by
the cardiograph: no hearsay evidence,
no incriminating script passes undetected.

All-night patrols keep you under surveillance,
permanent guard. Tomorrow, treated with

the deepest suspicion of malign behaviour,
you will be frisked for smuggled polyps, growths.

iv. Operation

After the endoscopic tests and X-rays,
the guilty verdict is pronounced.
Handcuffed to a metal intravenous stand,
you are escorted to the central operations room.

Your defence team briefs you on the nature
of the charges, your complete lack of immunity.
The futility of appeals. The special precautions
to be taken. In the event of. Just in case.

v. Textbook

The smaller the swelling the greater the danger.
Eighty percent are benign but surgery is always
advised, though removal poses a serious
risk of permanent damage to the facial nerve.

If not removed, there's a solid chance
the lump will prove eventually malignant.
If removed, it may grow back.
If malignant, it will almost certainly have spread.

vi. Broken Man

Smashed cars, scraped together in the salvage
yard, are scarred for life, shattered into
atoms of chromium and glass, too crushed
ever to qualify for roadworthiness again.

Your mind had suffered some unspeakable
collision, its impact written all over your face,
as if your brain were panel-beaten crudely
back to some simulacrum of normality.

VII. *Bandaged Heart*
    cast stainless steel by Cecily Brennan

The heart should be cast in steel
to spare it human feelings, wrapped
in a bow of bandages, a tourniquet to stem
the flow from blood-corroded arteries.

It is as if the heart had hardened
before its lava could yield up the molten
secrets of its chambers, congealing into
reflective metal, a love object of surgical steel.

VIII. **Analysis**

And who among the angelic orders will compensate
us for the gift of life? Who will make good our gains?
Who will be designated to help us come to terms
with the emotional strains of music we've endured?

How can we recover from the recurring attacks
of lovemaking we've known? What counselling
might reconcile us to our children's growing success,
allay the trauma of being spoilt for choice?

Meeting Points

You shake hands with fellow delegates
in the conference room, interpret the rakish
Italian's playful mime, swap business cards
and direct-line numbers with the Dane—
shirtsleeves ironed sharp as hatchet
blades—twiddling his country nameplate.
Once your final position on derogations
is sketched out with a plastic hotel pen,
the draft directive highlighted in Day-Glo lime,
no chairman's *tour de table* will faze you
when your time comes to answer for Ireland.

❧

Boarding at Brussels,
the Minister for Rural Development,
laptop strapped on shoulder,
is throatily feeding Gaelic
to a cell phone, having
taken his case to Europe.
Stooping below the awning
of the luggage rack,
the Minister for Agriculture
loosens his tie, settles back
for predinner aperitifs
and off-duty piss-taking
with his suited entourage.
Bliss. If only smoking
were still permissible.

❧

Another EU Working Group session in some
hosting Member State; another boardroom-style
layout in a hotel ballroom, the regulation baize
covering a multitude of joined-up trestles.
Eager microphones lean to overhear our
multilingual debate; the Chairman—clinking
a tumbler to call the room to order—makes
a start by summarising the agenda items.
En marge babble abates; backup staff
in the wings are busy with attendance sheets,
juggling departure details, airport taxi needs.
A revised draft directive is circulated, hot from
the photocopier like clothes folded from a drier.
An expert subgroup will surely be among
some delegation's proposals; for now,
the Chairman is kicking to touch, fielding
questions about the pie charts and graphs
that lend colour to his PowerPoint presentation.
Beyond the drawn velvet curtains, the gull
scream of a car alarm, the glassy rumpus
of empties from a passing brewery truck.

∼

Such happy release when,
the meeting having gone your way,
nothing added under AOB,

you scoop the briefing files
into your overnight valise, leaving
just enough spare time to grab

a magnum from duty-free,
claim your frequent flier miles,
beat the final boarding call.

You're not quite sure you've met; yet, some
pheromone of officialdom in the air
elicits a half nod from you as you pass:
your reflex reaction to his comparable suit
and tie; some hunch you may have faced
each other across a departmental table once,
partaken in a joint review group—who knows
what or when?—some confab or delegation
lost in a lifetime's fug of arbitrations, ordinances,
interagency liaison, temporising, files.

Back from a monitoring mission
          on best practice, you manipulate
the rigid key, snap cobwebs
          sealing the front door,
steal into the cool hall lit
          with a sallow long-life bulb
out of place in daylight,
          an addled firefly.
You punch in the alarm code
          to quell the piercing racket
of the control box,
          drag the mail-impeded door
wide enough to make space
          for your bags, manhandled
just now from the airport cab.

Fountain

It never rains but it pours.
Translate into heraldic Latin,
engrave onto the base of this public
    fountain which stores up untold
grudges, sculpted cups running over
    with angry outbursts, intense enough
to wring acidic tears from stone.
    Not a good word can it bring itself
to utter, spitting out vinegary grievances,
    spilling forth the messy details
in the language of the gutter. My God,
    how many sorrows there are
to drown once you get started.

Count your curses, it seems
    to say, *vows broken, illusions lost,*
ambitions thwarted. Let others gush.
    I am the one fountain, unbribable
with well-wishing coins, that cannot
    be bought off. The truth must out.
Mine is the no-nonsense voice
    for which false hopes will never wash;
in which you hear credence given
    to the fears you keep secreted
in your brain's innermost folds,
    its locked cells, woefully chanting
an unstoppable mantra:

Supposing. Supposing. Suppose...

Fifty O'Clock

Clearing out some boxes, the foxed *Guide to Life* comes as a shock. The section devoted to the sensuous mysteries well fingered in our youth. Can we have spread ourselves so far into its pages since then, slept together through whole chapters? How else might we have reached the years of anticlimax? How can we have arrived so soon at "Growing Old Gracefully"? What possible relevance does such a chapter hold for the young couple we have, for decades, been?

∽

Brokers, I notice, no longer proposition me with slinky proposals, glossy brochures offering to raise the level of my life cover "without need for medical examination."

∽

First reading glasses pinching my nose,
I peruse the small print of income continuance
plans, tax-efficient pension annuities,
practise the pronunciation of ailments—
reserved exclusively for over-fifties—
ending in *itis, osis, aemia.*

∽

Why the lights all night in the nursing home?
Is someone scared of ghosts?
The ghost of Christmas past or Christmas future?
The ghost in the mirror of the present tense?

∽

"I just never thought it would come so soon," my parents' youthful friend, Mary Olive, confessed from her hospice bed.

∼

During the halting funeral eulogy, a daughter
recalls her mother's circle of friends,
housewives whose dated names—Kitty, Sadie,
Bridie, Stasia—proclaim their era at an end.

∼

Inseparable, my body and I, till death us do part. Death, the bad company I'll fall in with, last thing my parents would have expected of me.

∼

Ah, but there's everything to play for yet, isn't there? Career shift. Holiday condo. Early retirement. Isn't there? You falter at a crossroads, the stake of a signpost rammed through its heart.

∼

And they too passed.
What was confided in low voices
on a homeward journey filtered back to air.
Their car was sold for scrap, for parts.
Cattle in roadside fields were fattened,
slaughtered, quartered, minced, consumed.
Pumps with slender metal taproots
made way for piped water.

∼

That I regret everything goes without saying.
What I did. What I didn't.

The time I bought. The time I sold.
Not to have waited. Not to have acted.
To have kept my mouth shut.
To have opened my big mouth.
To have taken it on the jaw.
Not to have turned the other cheek.
To be so weak. So headstrong.
That we didn't meet sooner.
That we met at all.
That I lived.
That I had to unlive.

∾

There you are in wedding day mode, Mother, sporting a rose ("A
rose upon a rose," my father rhapsodised): a young woman in
love, heart intent on starting a family.

∾

They bestowed rosebud hearts on children,
eyes and noses like family heirlooms,
ancestral expressions to which we now
bear helpless witness, each of us a photofit variation.

∾

And you really started something, Mother, when you indulged us
in creaming off the iron from your blood, siphoning it like red
diesel, harvesting your cells, cadging the calcium in your mouth
for our own selfish ends. Now cut to this photo of the family
reunion where we stuff our faces at a linen-vested table. What an
appetite for life you whetted in us.

∾

Life was all our ailing neighbour—not yet fifty—asked for.
And she'd snatch as much of it as could be spared.
Enough to see her to old age might do.
Just enough to last a lifetime would suffice.
It was life or nothing as far as she was concerned.
Let others take death lying down.
She was not, quite frankly, the dying type.
Never, ever would she stoop that low.

⌒

Think, even now, of all the wrong
turnings you will take before
you can call death your own.
All the decisions you will mess up.
All the blunders you will perpetrate.
Future remarks you'll want to retract.
Character flaws that magnify with
every passing year. Betrayals you'll
be in no position to deny.

⌒

Daydreaming, I imagine my entire life
still stacked in front of me like unspent cash,
as if some outrageous mistake had been made
in calculating my age and I could bring back
my birth cert like a receipt, insisting on a refund.

⌒

Mother, just the other day I thought of the perfume gift you came
to expect each year, until your fiftieth Christmas. What scent are
you on the trail of since then? Evening primrose spray? Black-
berried essence of belladonna, a nightshade fragrance?

after Hans Verhagen

A minute later, I noticed your breathing had stopped.
The autopsy recorded secondaries all over,
even in the farthest recesses of your lungs.
No wonder you were racked by such agonising spasms.
The miracle was that a ramshackle house
proved habitable so long.

Forever

Forever some customer happy to sing along with the supermarket Muzak, no matter how hackneyed or crass.

Forever the plangent sound of a motorcycle in the early hours, conjuring a world you once had access to.

Forever the young couple shutting the front door, leaving to conjecture what their next move may be.

Forever the van driver slowing down to check a house number against a delivery invoice.

Forever an old boy on a rickety bike with a loyal following of one terrier-type mongrel.

Forever the husband skulking outside the boutique while his wife seeks approval from a mirror.

Forever the kind who believe in God (a little) and horoscopes (a lot) and cannot resist a buy-one-get-one offer.

Forever those with a lump in the throat at every reconciliation scene, the theme music's pathos never failing to work its way straight to the left atrium of the heart.

Forever the cleaning woman tapping the pub window with a coin and the helmeted courier leaning his gob to the intercom.

Forever a caller so long on hold she wonders should she redial and brave the bossy touch-tone menu again.

Forever a youngster hacking the grass with bat or stick in what serves as a green space near the housing estate.

Forever, stopped in her tracks at One Hour Photo, a student smiling indulgently at her recent past.

Forever the secretary sprinting with franked mail to the post office, minutes before the closing curtain of steel shutters falls.

Forever, from an adjacent window, the commentator's animated voice as the ball approaches the goal area and lands: *I don't believe it...barely wide.*

Forever the widower turning up a Viennese polka on the Sunday morning programme and scribbling "Slovak Radio Symphony Orchestra" on a phone bill.

Forever the girl upending the nearly empty crisp packet and savouring life to the full, to the last salty cheese-and-onion-flavoured crumb.

Forever the old ladies who smile at babies like politicians and suspect the meter reader may not really be the meter reader.

Forever a freckled builder in high-vis jacket swinging his lunch bag as he clocks in at the chipboard hoarding.

Forever the teenagers who can't pass up a hat display without trying on preposterous headgear in a department store.

Forever the tall schoolboy with ponytail and full-length leather coat. And forever the small one, pate shaved almost bald, nursing a cigarette like a sore finger.

Forever the sort who texts a request for her boyfriend to the lunchtime show—then throws in a greeting to her aunt and uncle, just for the heck.

Forever the thickset woman, dragging a shopping trolley, who pauses to rub a lottery scratch card like Aladdin's lamp.

Forever the exasperated mother—hatchback open, hazards flashing, eyes peeled for the traffic police—while her son, packing the drum kit, plays it cool.

Forever the laughter fading, a dropped coin spinning to a wobbly stop.

Forever life heading about its business in places vaguely familiar, like an ex-weatherwoman's face, a New Zealand premier's name.

Forever. And ever. All going well.

Ever After

Whatever construction we put on
the mortification of the flesh by death,
whatever the happy-clappy euphemisms
we choose to shroud its devastation with,

there are few enough consoling glosses
to be put on a body scrapped in
tamped-down clay, trampled underfoot,
so reduced in means as to be human

infill, biodegrading fast, depreciation
setting in unless disposed of smartly.
We joke about it all, fall back
on bad puns, black humour,

wanting to sidestep negative
insinuations, stay true to the living
body, fend off morbidity, sublimate
our dread, stuff the unsettling

dead back into their crumbling boxes,
keep the snuff of their rancid dust from
getting up our noses, install granite
headstones to pin them firmly down.

There Was

there was a house
wood-smoke was part of it
drinking water rinsed in peat
trace elements of cloves and sage
December light was in it
grey as a collared dove

spontaneous gatherings
of rainwater
were funnelled down
the gullies of the sloping lane

above the hooked cooking utensils
on the open hearth
the kitchen chimney made
a lookout post from which
you monitored the sky
that sad-eyed creature
outdoors in all weathers
brushed with mushy cloud

there was a moment
it had a waftage of frankincense
logs came from a toppled trunk
your uncle dragged bodily
from the hilltop forest
like the antlered stag
its mounted head still flaunted in the hall
opposite the mildewed looking glass
that tarnished everyone alike

antler leaves defended holly beads
the fuchsia bush beside the roughcast wall
had stood the test of eternity

each summer robbing nests
laid-back cuckoos
made their eggs at home
in the forest where your barefoot
father's school carved out
a limestone eyrie among the trees
my god talk about wildflowers mosses fungi ferns
rustlings from undergrowth stirrings from burrows
tracks and pawmarks badger setts fox scents unlikely birds

you gasped a little at whatever
it was you had within your grasp
clutched it as best you could
sensed its closeness as you passed
the rosewood cabinet from which
an illustrated *Christmas Carol*
—with gilded cover blizzard—
had been removed

brothers sister two girl cousins
played with board games crayons
winds whining outside
answered to a different world
and the mud-clobbered yard
was revealed only to make
the timbered parlour floor
even more secure under your feet
its heat more precious

unthinkable that your parents
would ever need to retrace
the drab miles home
that your uncle might step
out into that faltering day
with hay or mangels for the cattle

and something in the moment
was brighter for the darkness
warmer for the storm putting pressure
on the rowan tree in the rushy field
more reliable for the tiny squared-off
windowpanes in which the scene
was compressed into eye-sized segments

the latch rattles in the flagstoned kitchen
a whispered mist of smoke is picked up
a disturbed log sleeping on the job
buds suddenly into orange squash-coloured flames

a dusk chorus of voices
none at cross purposes for once
you know from the tone
everyone is in complete agreement
the details can be thrashed out later
meanwhile tea and lemonade are poured
iced tar-black slices passed around

you are clinging
to the candlelit moment
holding its trusted hand
tightly as a flame
attaches to a wick

shake the day
it might start snowing
like this water globe:
a glass-cocooned nativity
you agitate—
blocked salt cellar—
letting loose its grains
on the stable that could easily
be the rattling zinc-roofed
cattle shed outside

snow lodging
in that yard
would never melt

Miłosz's Return

I searched for it, found it, recognized it.

Czesław Miłosz, "A Meadow"

The field your memory singled out for
special treatment can be located by you still:

the one the sun would always make
an extra fuss about, buff until it gleamed

like a copper pan suspended in the oak-
beamed kitchen of your manor house.

Retrace the well-worn path of memory.
Nothing is beyond recovery. No one has died.

For, as you yourself have prophesied,
The rivers will return to their beginnings...

The dead will wake up, not comprehending.
Till everything that happened has unhappened.

Unlatch the gate. Lean against the haystack.
Look where you were taken by her lips.

Where the horse-drawn rake, weeds
stuck between its teeth, was rusting.

Where a cow stood ruminating over
sow thistles or in hock to clover and buttercup.

Where the acquisitive bees made a dash
for the linden grove and light filled in

the gaps between the apple trees.
Where heart-fluttering butterflies clapped wings.

Where green hay, toppled by scythes, soaked up
heat like berries ripening for preserves.

Home in time, you find your bearings there
among sweet calamus and whirring snipe.

PART TWO

Skywriting

The sky leaves every possibility wide open,
its wraparound screen receptive to
any scene unfolding on its surface:
constellations fluttering in cosmic gales,
planes plying trade routes across continents,
shooting stars detached like retinas,
sun rays adding decorative motifs.
Primed with a wash of nothingness,
it can stretch its flexible canvas
as far as distance permits,
vanishing point infinitely elusive.

∽

Darkness is what mainly marks
these muckraking winter Saturdays
that never quite get off the ground,
becoming bogged down in cloud.
And, at the time of morning when you'd
rather have a lawnmower up and running
or a paint can open like a puree,
torpor permeates your pores,
blackens your soul like the coal lumps
you work up to a heated exchange.
Best to abandon the fight, give up the ghost.
Best to let the darkness have its day.

∽

Endlessly pliable, the sky draws out
its substance in every direction, a ductile
metal thinned almost to invisibility
but tinged at dawn with finger-painted limes,

cornelians and iodines, canned-salmon pinks.
Vein of skimmed-milk blue, font of impermanent
inks, if not clotting into creamy cloud
it soon assumes a pure cerulean
that saturates space without a join or seam,
its uninterrupted stream of consciousness
a testament to life lived outside of time.

Light shimmies down this high-rise
art museum to the busy street below,
slipping into any gap that leaves itself
exposed to the benign influence of sun,
dips a flickering toe in the fountain
at the park, coaxes dark trees to lighten up.
The window cleaner of a nearby building pauses
at its forty-second floor, checks his watch, stares earthward,
platform dangling like the basket of an air balloon.
He might be a farmer leaning on a rail fence,
taking stock, squinting across a prospect
of ploughed fields—remoulded drills—
where secreted wheat will be revealed.
Or even, were it day's end, this Edward Hopper
filling station owner, totting his paltry sales
in the frail illumination of his gas pumps:
fir trees plot behind his back to soak in
darkness like carbon dioxide and his
secluded stretch of road runs dangerously
low in light, gauge zeroing in on EMPTY.

It must drive you to despair, living always under
leaden skies, a sheltering tourist—transparent
mac over zipped anorak—will propose when

louring clouds conspire with rain; faces give way
to umbrellas navigating down the showery street.
And we agree, as we can hardly not, wet rot
attacking attics, rain entering our bloodstreams.
Yet we have an understanding with the weather:
whenever squalls end and sun returns with
friendly fire, we would forgive it anything.
It resembles Friday evenings then, the grind
of the working week almost worthwhile
for the exhilaration freedom brings by contrast.
And if a rainbow's spray-painted sash is added,
the chemistry between us is a perfect match—
fidelity rewarded, reconciliation complete.

A winter dawn, struggling to shake off
the blacker aspects of the night,
keeps its sleeping inhabitants in the dark.
Sandy beaches take in water: a sleet-chilled
high-salt muddy-coloured mushroom broth.
In lakeside cottages with empty bunk beds
timer switches activate a lightbulb rota.
Snow, unseen, rears up on mountains.
What a heroic profile Earth presents,
holding its own against the serried might
of galaxies, the flight of migrating comets,
resisting the tug of antiparticles,
the desolation of black holes.

True, as friends say cheerily, *it will*
be all the same to you in a thousand years.
But now, right now, it matters greatly
to the small-brained, species-centred,

peer-influenced creature you are.
Joy, glimpsed like a long-tailed comet,
keeps on eluding you: too remote for
the naked eye to know whether that
distant glimmer moves infinitesimally
closer or is spluttering further away.
In either case, it will not cross your
flight path in any foreseeable future.
Meanwhile, taking a dim view of
the present, you come down to earth
with an awful lot of explaining to do.

Such an old stalwart, the sun,
always rising to the occasion,
never missing a day, raising crops
of maize to ripeness, rounding melons,
tenderising pears, lending bounce
to black-tipped hooves of lambs,
adding layers of intrigue and silence
to dirt roads wandering off the map.
And, as if that were not bounty enough,
it masters the art of penetrating glass,
brings a glint to every facet of a fruit bowl,
causes the vase of dahlias in the framed
still life to waver: our house elevated
above its station, pitched at the level
of a Dutch interior, lives clarified by light.

You can see so much in the dark of night—
even more than that paw-swinging cat does,
marching along its beat, as you watch
raindrop equations repeat to infinity

on the window when you rise at three to suss out
some sound you think you may have heard.
You are breaking bad news to yourself—a cold
arctic glow, an aurora borealis of home truths—
with the full disclosure darkness stipulates.
Heartless rains resume thrashing the glass
as the planet continues its orbit into dawn;
one of its travel-sick crew, you find its universal
implications greater than you can grasp,
a yawning enormity kept in check by clouds.

I want it to be not just summer but May:
horizons broadening, light expanding by the day.
Not just May but warm, the slightest brush
with sunlight accelerating germination.
Not just warm but bright. Not just bright but blue.
Blue as hectares of bluebells hewn from the air.
Blue as the air itself.

Morning incites the sun to make up
for ground lost overnight... Light starts
exalting high-rise buildings, spreading
its growth-promoting warmth where
not even hardy weeds subsist, until settling
on a stunted grove of conifers in tubs
at a roof garden's fountain-oozing terrace.
Scaling the stairs of windows, step by step,
it takes hotel personnel by surprise
as they prepare the breakfast buffet
in the executive suite: tan cereals,
crustaceous croissants, fanned-out slices
of cooked meats, bowls of dismembered

grapefruits; it seeps into depopulated
office blocks, where workers will teem later,
gannets clinging to a precipitous existence.

ༀ

A glow-in-the-dark night. Radio telescopes
craning to catch reverberations from the universe.
The sky is the one absolute: there is no
gainsaying the truths it tells, pegged out
spaciously in constellations that pinpoint our
locations when we find ourselves at sea;
stars dazzling with the import of stale
news travelling from millennia ago.
Yet, gravitating back in cosmic time,
we know the lure of obscure objects
too: poke about black holes,
explore dark matter for our origins.

ༀ

How dull the world would be without
its shadows. How unjust. Nothing
to attenuate the harsher sentiments
of noon, sun pushing its weight around,
having it all its own way: no second side
to any story; no keeping time with a garden's
limestone sundial; nothing to tap the darker
undercurrents, the bass notes; nothing
to restore some balance to the picture.
Grant us more sun so that there may
be shadows in abundance: tenaciously
faithful to every step we take, they
are wrenched from the world only when
we rise above it, jet engines muscling
their way skyward, upwardly mobile,

the plane's earthbound double in
hot pursuit, desperately scrambling
to keep pace, like a waving child
who chases a cousin's departing car.

On midwinter day, sun excavates
the entrances of passage tombs,
surveys their corbelled vaults, revives
their spirits with a light touch.
And slabs of weather-beaten stone—
wedged on heathery mountaintops
that offer panoramas of five fertile counties—
carrying boulders like the weight
of the world on granite shoulders,
receive a warm overspill of light,
as do these giant incisors—a ring of
standing stones—which form a sun trap.

The day is in the clear. Suds of mist
have shifted stains of darkness, purified the air.
More spacious now, spring-cleaned
of detritus, the sky is testing its endurance
to the limit, extending its remit.
April's message sinks in everywhere,
penetrating even to the densest levels
of dowdy brown clay, inaugurating
a flurry of buds and blossoms.
A tortoiseshell comes out of hiding,
wings blinking in the light; in the warm
colours of a day it would be a gross
betrayal to kill off, a squandering
of early promise for a still-unravelling

narrative that, so far, has no end in sight.
Refusing to go down without a fight, the sun
will make an exit, stage west, its reds
spreading like wildfire as though everything
remaining had been set alight and the sky
were a backdrop fabricated from flammable
material that had burst into flame.

∽

The sun throws light
on this morning's light,
as if a weight of clouds
had lifted from the day
or someone tripped a switch:
even the last flaky scrap
rusting in a ditch breaks
into a captivating shine.

∽

No one can look at death or the sun
without being left entirely in the dark.
Nor, with impunity, may the sun
expect to gaze directly at the moon.
Awestruck birds, fallen silent
before totality, know this when
the sun, corona blazing, is deposed.
Blossoms close up shop; nocturnal
moths report for duty; metal-plated
echo-sounding bats might strike out
any moment. A suspenseful chill
creeps across the gawking crowds.
Keeping sparks of hope alive, starlight
gouges airholes in the untimely night.

The sun, in shining form, raises office
morale, hints at a day that has been
scrubbed down, sandblasted like a sooty
building, smartened with a facelift.
To the tip of my tongue comes the old
chestnut about a stretch being noticeable...
But my desk pad's *November* interrupts
with a reminder that the year must contract
further, keep its pact with darkness, that
—contrary to appearances—this buoyant
example of dayhood is limping into port.

Streamlined blues as far as the eye
can see. Which is not very far.
Only as far as the next smoke screen
of cloud or the sunset you are warned,
on pain of blindness, to turn aside from.
Whatever truth lies at the back of that beyond
stays strictly classified, out of bounds: your
frontier is a sky awash with frothy constellations;
sun and moon like eyes in an old master portrait
that follow you inscrutably around a room.

Reiterating whatever claim it makes,
a sotto voce repetition, rain plays out
a reverie-inducing music on the glass
harmonica of the kitchen's windowpane.
But, peeling open the back door
for a rain check, you hear the liquid
swishing grow insistent as a whip;

sibilant drips insinuate their way
between tightly packed leaves which,
gorging on these waters, never
quite reach saturation point.
Hard to imagine that sweetness
and light might yet triumph,
a freshly perfumed day resurface,
put on airs of mellowness,
a rose-tinted sun assume the contours
of a mountain range, your gable wall.

❧

Stillest of Sundays in the village.
You leap ashore into a light
finely spun as fishing line.
The lake comes to with little
fits and starts: sun makes a play
for its impressionable surface,
rays splashing out in all directions.
Decked in sandals, shorts,
you amble down to check
if anyone's awake to rustle up
some breakfast egg and bacon
at the Lakeview Café's mess.

❧

Heat abrades the layers of cloud.
Token fronds of cumulus remaining
are an ornamental garnish, setting off
the sun, trapping twilit juices later
the way swordfish takes its flavour
from a bay leaf and basil marinade.
A pinch of stars will serve as seasoning.
Moon lights up from a stub of sun.

A rainbow is frescoed
on the back wall of the sky:
a sky that will digest its iridescence,
wash it down with rain.

What a show the sun puts on,
performing like a star,
raining spotlight beams,
cutting out behind a cloud
before—stunt pilot—
revving up its light again.
Or watch its sleight of hand,
its stagy way of conjuring
a coruscating day from mist,
holding it in abeyance,
under wraps—a slow burner—
until the timing is exactly right
(fields hazy about their parts,
birds shuffling in the wings);
then, with a rising degree
of intensity, it blends tar's
redolence with the usual
fragrances—petunia, rose,
mown hay—and refreshes
spellbinding memories
of when there was no
limit to the sky and our
horizons knew no bounds.

Moonlight colludes with churchyard yews
to sketch a spectral scene. Weathered headstones,
brought to life, seem to lean back with
brash attitude: a goth band's glowering
entourage on an album-cover photo shoot.
Eldritch beams slip in between the bedroom
curtains, a stalactite sliver of shivery light,
cold as the loner's shot of midnight gin
nipped from the minibar of a cheap hotel
on which the darkness confers stars.

❧

Come sunset these evenings,
cloud banks—firmly shut till then—
open like clockwork, as if
operated by a time lock.
The golden coin that spills out
is donated too late to save
the day; shops closing,
commuters flocking underground.
No time remains to catch
these last-minute offers of light.

❧

Through old elastic-stockinged
aspens with the shakes I glimpse
the sky in pristine nick, as if toxic
smoke had never wafted its way,
planes had never scrawled graffiti
contrails on its glass. Those mountain
peaks, plastered with newly minted snow,
that could be the illustration on a tin
of breath fresheners will be haloed
at sunset with a violet otherworldly rim.

Not a blot on the sky's escutcheon.
Not a cloud on the sea's horizon.
Sea and sky are indivisible here,
invisibly threaded together, blue to blue,
the seam that separates them
barely traceable by the eye.
Then *sunset and evening star.*
Darkness enters cagily, goes against
our wishes, over our heads, flecks
of paradisal plumage showing
through the closing bars of sky.
The day peters out, having, for one day
only, made its countrywide appearance.
Twilight and evening bell,
And after that the dark.

Lavish with light, sagging under its own
proliferating weight, the harvest moon
staggers above a mountain, heaves
itself up, hacks through darkness, finding
room for manoeuvre at the apex of the sky,
challenging the sun's monopoly, skimming
off a wattage of its purest energy, sloshing
about in cloud, filtering like blue gaslight
through glass. Mezzotint lakes, enamelled
rivers glinting with a fish-scale silver,
flaking trees, antique hand-coloured
gardens: a world engraved in steel.
Other nights, the moon behaves more
intimately, lowering its sights: a lamp
suspended above a table in a family-run
bistro known only to a lucky few.

⌒⌣

I dream a sky cobbled with bombers,
armour-plated with parked planes,
fuselages nose-to-tail; a tongued
and grooved planetary roof
proofed against sun's infiltration.

⌒⌣

The pale winter sun is trying to take off
into the wild blue yonder, but its light
lacks staying power; evening—seeking
closure—soon calls it a day.
The one gaping hole still leaking low-level
light, weak as a butane-fuelled ring
on a windy picnic site, is patched over
quickly, airbrushed from the record,
and a united front of darkness presented:
tight-lipped, admitting no dissent; leaving
the starkest possible options to creatures
retorting with feeble reading lamps
and watchful halogens; challenging
frantic eyes to identify a single
resistant pocket, a last defiant reserve.

⌒⌣

Winter 1957. Stars strung out like fairy lights.
We stood our garden's ground until the Sputnik
satellite came round to our ways: a sidereal
blip, *a one-eyed yellow idol* of technology.
All across the island, shivering families warred
against the cold; pyjamas under gabardines,
we lined the astral route, waving the flashy
object onward, rewarded with a cursory wink.

Eyes drawn to dizzy heights of stars,
I tried to join their puzzling dots.

Late autumn light, bronze as beech leaves,
terminates at my office desk, aggrandising
my memos, gilding the journeyman prose
of my draft chairman's speech, making
copperplate of briefing papers on compliance
costs, leaning across my coffinwood press,
weakly stooping at an awkward angle,
casting the room in sepia, dispensing
with my presence, pensioning me off.

As your transatlantic flight nears home, clouds
surround the coastline, tidemarks around a bath.
Vacation over too soon, worries pester you again.
The welcome is subdued, scumbled sunlight less
than overwhelming in its warmth when you descend
—backpack, T-shirt, trainers—from the dishevelled cabin
to the tarmac smarting from an outburst of recent rain.

The afternoon lapses into the background
as its shimmering surface holds sway,
making the still moment a mirage of itself,
baking it into memory, an infrangible clay.
Draped across stone steps, sun glorifies
the torpid gravel, shows up a whitewashed
courtyard, imbues a hedge with light
entwined so ardently with every leaf
you must avert your dazzled eyes.

A wasp's narcotic soundtrack amplifies.
It is all beyond belief.

∽

We've lived under a cloud all winter,
uniformly grey, like small print
setting out warranty restrictions.
Now a shiny new day dawns,
luminous as ice in a champagne bucket.
Ozone's sunscreen melting, will we
weary of displays of solar might?:
fearing its heat monotonously
bearing down, invading our
space, always butting in,
hogging every conversation,
making us sweat it out,
casting a stifling shadow
on our lives, febrile brains
fantasising about sleet and snow,
olden days when skies pencilled in
a fence of charcoal cloud
and a mild sun beamed benignly
through random slats, rays
dusting rain-irrigated crops.

∽

Abandoning the peat-scented heat in which
fireside chairs nested, we blunder towards the car
parked where the farmyard light runs out
and night sets about its work in earnest.
A lamp's beam would only bounce off
the solid black substance that engulfs us,
increase our sense of inconsequence when
up against colossal odds of time and space.

Spreading wind-borne rumours, pine trees
taunt with the doom-laden prophecies
of graveyard yews. A few low-grade stars:
too far away to comfort or shed light.

Whatever pious upward-gazing
eyes once saw in the sky's reredos
has become a blur, the apocalyptic
light of dusk—wines, divine golds,
daubs of ceremonial purples:
colours mixed in the sun's image
like the abstract canvases we stand
in awe of at a gallery's sanctuary,
as though waiting for the heavens
to open and the veils of our temples
to be rent with intensity of vision.

These wintry evenings, the moon—pale
undertaker—shows up with indecent haste,
ushering away the day's remains as soon
as the sun shows signs of wasting, turning cold.
Trees and hedges reduced to squiggles, a rough
sketch, it's back to the drawing board for nature.
In fairness, the vigilant moon keeps its flame
discreetly burning into dawn when the irruption
of a thrush, finding its voice again, lends a certain
splendour to the morning: a wake-up call,
ruffling the feathers of the incoming day, fluffing
them up like the clay in this newly harrowed land.

For as long as the sun can hold its
dominating role, there will be beauty
of a kind: the kind that turns the tide
of rain, trapped on a flat warehouse roof,
into calm seas dipped in syrupy light,
putting the musty word *refulgent* through
its paces, its meaning given a new gloss.
Mosses invade a rooftop overflow tank
like sea lettuce wading a rockpool;
and the ball cock makes a striped beach ball
drifting distantly away under the dreamy
no-cloud sky of an essay on school hols.

Summers after work we drive out to take
the light, burrowing through gilt-edged
tree tunnels, emerging to fields and hedges
shown to best advantage in the evening sun,
delighting in a realm of pure contingency
where every vital detail is left to chance,
light freely associating with gradient of hill
and radiance of rock, arranging serendipitous
meetings of stocky sheep and elongating
shadows, sweeping over obsolete machines
in ramshackle farmyards, permeating lanes.
Sun visors down like knights,
we fend off winter for another day.

Having tapped in the alarm code,
like clearing passport control,
I linger at my open doorway,
standing in the sun's light,
blocking its path, knocking

a man-size dent in its rays
while shamelessly poaching
whatever heat I get away with.
What was it I needed to attend to
urgently as soon as I came home?
Immobilised by light, I find my
place in the sun, transported by
this unexpected stroke of luck.

Nights don't come much blacker
than this, backup lighting of moon
and stars having failed to generate.
Every trace of life obliterated, you are
up against the ends of the earth.

Somewhere the rush of spring-water.
Somewhere the excavator yellow of furze bushes.
A laburnum resurgence sighted through a pergola.
Unimpeded light—every pore translucent—recalling
an age when the sun looked indulgently on a world
in its prime, a planet slanted in favour of its rays
yet unable to absorb so much illumination at one time.

While your mother furls the blind, pulsating
sun sneaks in behind her to your sickroom,
underlines the midmorning peculiarity
of a day off school, an uncanny stillness.
Chest of drawers and wardrobe reverberate
with light as the thermometer advances
a further notch, like a child's height chart.

She settles the bedclothes crisply,
straightens the candlewick quilt, bolsters
starched pillows, and leaves you
with an aftertaste of cough potion,
drowsing in her shadow; woozily paging
your favourite comic; doused in tonic light.

∿

January: the zealous moon outshines
everything for miles, out on its own
despite a full complement of stars.
By morning, though, it is a burned-out
case; a car's frosted windshield;
the ceiling cobweb a brush with
the wing of a migrant goose would
sweep away; a plaster death mask.
Now jets are sketching trails
in vapour, their lines the shortest
distances between two cities.
To no great avail, a wintry sun—
splinter of ice in its heart—makes
a stolid showing above a fresh,
unyielding pelt of settled snow.

∿

An Indian summer in late September
stretches the definition of the season
well beyond what's strictly reasonable,
conceding the latitude everyone—no matter
what their age—relaxing at those pavement café
tables pleads for secretly when the appellation
young is doled out casually in conversation.
The sun enjoys its final fling, a last fine careless
rapture, burning its midday oil, as a throbbing

love song hovers above an open sports car.
Living for the present, putting all thoughts
of a rainy day on hold, friends catch the waiter's
eye for a latte top-up or a half-carafe of red.

∽

Enhancing the landscape like a soft-focus lens,
a winter mist restores the world this early morning
to its pastoral phase, harmonising clashing colours,
breaking down barriers between field and road
and forest, laminating mountains, sealing in their
freshness, our landfill waste and quarried devastation
vaporised, industrial estates proving biodegradable.
Even the power cables—straight as potato drills—
might be the threads binding the whole narrative
web together, spinning out the seasonal cycle
for a further 1,001 days, or however long it can—
without sagging or faltering—still be credibly sustained.

∽

To hold a waxed orange is to play with fire,
to watch a blazing torch annihilate the darkness,
lending you the night vision of a marmalade cat.
Best of all possible worlds, its fleece-lined inner
skin is warm even to the eye; it worships light without
the swivelling sunflower's anxious scouring of the sky.
Remove one citrus grove from the picture and you
cave in to dark forces, extinguish brightest hopes.

∽

Clouds in tatters. The sky fragmented,
shattered dramatically into a million
wads of colour. A thin veneer of cumuli

appears for all the world to be an inverted
beach, tropical sands at sunset,
the kind of resort that travel
brochures invariably dub *unspoilt.*
And though it's morning here, not night,
cold not hot—trees redefined by mist,
delicately nuanced hills, brittle,
vitreous, icy grass—the sky paints
a different picture, totally over the top,
laying on molten reds with a palette knife.
The day is dead. Long live the day.
Things hang in the balance for a minute,
the sun itself unsure how the near future
might pan out but already scheming
to leave early, abandon this morning's
potential, slink away at the first sign
of evening's narrower horizon kicking in
to cut off the last escape hatch that remains.

∾

A rainbow tacked onto the sky—
fridge magnet, temporary tattoo,
crèche logo—has a way of prompting
primitive responses, adding a dash
of complication to the world,
redolent of those incongruities
we do our best to explain away
through open-and-shut laws
of cosmology which keep reopening;
doors of perception that bang on
in the draughty outbacks of infinity,
the awkward gaps between the stars.

∾

Though winter starts to clamp down
on the light, enforcing a curfew earlier
every night, yet sun salvages something
of its former power, however tentatively,
on crisp December days, its clarity
cutting no ice, but slicing through
the human clutter nonetheless:
making its mark as a bright patch
perking up some aftermath
to the freshness of organic salad leaves.
On the overshadowed lawn its calling card
is a fluorescent beam that leads
the whole way to the garden wall
and seems to touch its red brick with
inklings of a realm to which it offers
wider access, operating outside of time's
laws, moonlighting on eternity's behalf.

What I remember of the place is light:
its plenitude; how fairly it was distributed
across wheat-thatched fields given the run
of the country without the impediment
of a single hindering hedge;
brilliance so profuse that sunflowers
could not decide which way to turn.
Fluctuating butterflies, light on their feet,
fanned themselves against the summer
heat; bees rounded on lavender spikes
like harvest mice gnawing corn;
and, in a dusty lane under cover
of staggeringly leafy plane trees,
old men stooped to deal out metal spheres.
When sun had sunk to dusk level,

voices resounded from pavement cafés,
nectarine-screened courtyards, shuttered houses.
Sounds—wineglass chimes, clangs
of cutlery on plates, animated conversations
—jolted me back from reverie in my *pension:*
words impacting on each other
like the tiny metal dents left in lethargic
afternoons when *boules* collide.

∿

Tailgated by stars, the long-haul plane loses
its battle against the dark: passengers too on
autopilot, cabin lights are dimmed, gibberish
drones through slippage of in-flight headphones.
Yet, all this time, resistance mounts; overwhelming
any final judgement, a rim of light—glimmer
of optimism—appears from nowhere, the sky
running ahead of bleary eyes as breakfast trays
are served, stars brushed away like crumbs.

∿

Playing a disappearing trick
on the freeze-framed, heat-stilled day,
Seurat's paint becomes so light
it evaporates into its own haze,
atomises, breaks up like an
out-of-range phone conversation;
stippled grains that could be
tossed around on any breeze:
flecks of coastal sand,
unseasonable motes of snow.

∿

Desiccated, dry-as-dust, powder-puff fields.
Scorched earth. There is change in the air,
some shift in the balance of planetary power:
trees strain at the leash of hurricanes, ground
battles deplete plant and insect stockpiles.
The tide turns in the sea's favour:
oceans burst their banks, glaciers snap,
ice caps retreat, meltwaters run like pus.
The world is too much in the sun.
Now the heat is on, threatening meltdown.
We who seized on the spark of promise
in drowned peat, mined coal seams
to stoke up neon signs, squeezed mileage
allowances from refined petroleum, leave
our carbon footprints on the sands of time,
anoint machines with oils: driving a hard bargain;
wanting the sun, moon, and stars; sure our
fossil-fuelled journeys through congested
dusks will lead as ever to a renovated dawn.

Think of a number. Double it.
Multiply that, for argument's sake,
by some astronomical figure to find
the rate at which the universe
is speeding into pieces or how many
depleted stars are concentrated
into ravenous black holes.
Round up the answer with your
calculating mind as you try to come
to terms with zeroes lined up to infinity:
so many light-years for truth to dawn,
so many theories of dark matter,
so many millennia until night falls

on our universe and everything
on earth comes down to nothing—
like nothing on earth you could
imagine in a billion years.

～

Difficult to second-guess what might
happen next, what climate of fear
we have coming to us in the future.
But, over today's horizon, May
appears in perfect working order,
seen in the best possible light;
bringing out the colour in furze bushes,
granting leaves a seasonal reprieve.
Butterflies contrive a soft landing
on extravagant polyanthus.
Grain shoots are gaining ground.
Sprays of rowan disperse scent.
And a still-gentle sun caresses
the brow of the hill: a cow
licking her newborn calf.

ABOUT THE AUTHOR

Dennis O'Driscoll was born in Thurles, County Tipperary, Ireland, in 1954. His eight books of poetry include *Weather Permitting* (Anvil Press Poetry, 1999), which was a Poetry Book Society Recommendation and short-listed for the *Irish Times* Poetry Prize; *Exemplary Damages* (Anvil, 2002); and *New and Selected Poems* (Anvil, 2004), a Poetry Book Society Special Commendation. His work is included in *The Wake Forest Series of Irish Poetry*, Volume 1 (Wake Forest University Press, 2005).

A selection of his essays and reviews, *Troubled Thoughts, Majestic Dreams* (Gallery Books), was published in 2001. He is editor of the *Bloodaxe Book of Poetry Quotations* (Bloodaxe Books, 2006) and its American counterpart, *Quote Poet Unquote: Contemporary Quotations on Poets and Poetry* (Copper Canyon Press, 2008). *Stepping Stones: Interviews with Seamus Heaney* (Farrar, Straus and Giroux) was published in 2008.

O'Driscoll received a Lannan Literary Award in 1999, the E.M. Forster Award from the American Academy of Arts and Letters in 2005, and the O'Shaughnessy Award for Poetry from the Center for Irish Studies in 2006.

A member of Aosdána, the Irish academy of artists, he has worked as a civil servant since the age of sixteen.

Copper Canyon Press gratefully acknowledges
Lannan Foundation for supporting the publication and
distribution of exceptional literary works.

LANNAN LITERARY SELECTIONS 2008

Lars Gustafsson, *A Time in Xanadu*

David Huerta, *Before Saying Any of the Great Words: Selected Poetry*

Sarah Lindsay, *Twigs and Knucklebones*

Valzhyna Mort, *Factory of Tears*

Dennis O'Driscoll, *Reality Check*

LANNAN LITERARY SELECTIONS 2000–2007

Maram al-Massri, *A Red Cherry on a White-tiled Floor: Selected Poems*, translated by Khaled Mattawa

Marvin Bell, *Rampant*

Hayden Carruth, *Doctor Jazz*

Cyrus Cassells, *More Than Peace and Cypresses*

Madeline DeFrees, *Spectral Waves*

Norman Dubie
The Insomniac Liar of Topo
The Mercy Seat: Collected & New Poems, 1967–2001

Sascha Feinstein, *Misterioso*

James Galvin, *X: Poems*

Jim Harrison, *The Shape of the Journey: New and Collected Poems*

Hồ Xuân Hương, *Spring Essence: The Poetry of Hồ Xuân Hương*, translated by John Balaban

June Jordan, *Directed by Desire: The Collected Poems of June Jordan*

Maxine Kumin, *Always Beginning: Essays on a Life in Poetry*

Ben Lerner, *The Lichtenberg Figures*

Antonio Machado, *Border of a Dream: Selected Poems*, translated by Willis Barnstone

W.S. Merwin
The First Four Books of Poems
Migration: New & Selected Poems
Present Company

Taha Muhammad Ali, *So What: New & Selected Poems, 1971–2005,*
translated by Peter Cole, Yahya Hijazi, and Gabriel Levin

Pablo Neruda
The Separate Rose, translated by William O'Daly
Still Another Day, translated by William O'Daly

Cesare Pavese, *Disaffections: Complete Poems 1930–1950,*
translated by Geoffrey Brock

Antonio Porchia, *Voices,* translated by W.S. Merwin

Kenneth Rexroth, *The Complete Poems of Kenneth Rexroth*

Alberto Ríos
The Smallest Muscle in the Human Body
The Theater of Night

Theodore Roethke
On Poetry & Craft: Selected Prose of Theodore Roethke
Straw for the Fire: From the Notebooks of Theodore Roethke

Benjamin Alire Sáenz, *Dreaming the End of War*

Rebecca Seiferle, *Wild Tongue*

Ann Stanford, *Holding Our Own: The Selected Poems of Ann Stanford*

Ruth Stone, *In the Next Galaxy*

Joseph Stroud, *Country of Light*

Rabindranath Tagore, *The Lover of God,* translated by Tony K. Stewart
and Chase Twichell

Reversible Monuments: Contemporary Mexican Poetry,
edited by Mónica de la Torre and Michael Wiegers

César Vallejo, *The Black Heralds,* translated by Rebecca Seiferle

Eleanor Rand Wilner, *The Girl with Bees in Her Hair*

Christian Wiman, *Ambition and Survival: Becoming a Poet*

C.D. Wright
One Big Self: An Investigation
Steal Away: Selected and New Poems

Matthew Zapruder, *The Pajamaist*

The Chinese character for poetry is made up of two parts: "word" and "temple." It also serves as pressmark for Copper Canyon Press.

Since 1972, Copper Canyon Press has fostered the work of emerging, established, and world-renowned poets for an expanding audience. The Press thrives with the generous patronage of readers, writers, booksellers, librarians, teachers, students, and funders—everyone who shares the belief that poetry is vital to language and living.

Major funding has been provided by:

Anonymous (2)

Beroz Ferrell & The Point, LLC

Lannan Foundation

National Endowment for the Arts

Cynthia Lovelace Sears and Frank Buxton

Washington State Arts Commission

For information and catalogs:

COPPER CANYON PRESS

Post Office Box 271

Port Townsend, Washington 98368

360-385-4925

www.coppercanyonpress.org

The text for this book is Minion, with titles set in DIN Engschrift. Book design and composition by Phil Kovacevich. Printed on archival-quality paper at McNaughton & Gunn, Inc.